14 Cows

FOR AMERICA

IN COLLABORATION WITH

Wilson Kimeli Naiyomah

14 Cows
FOR AMERICA

Carmen Agra Deedy

ILLUSTRATED BY

Thomas Gonzalez

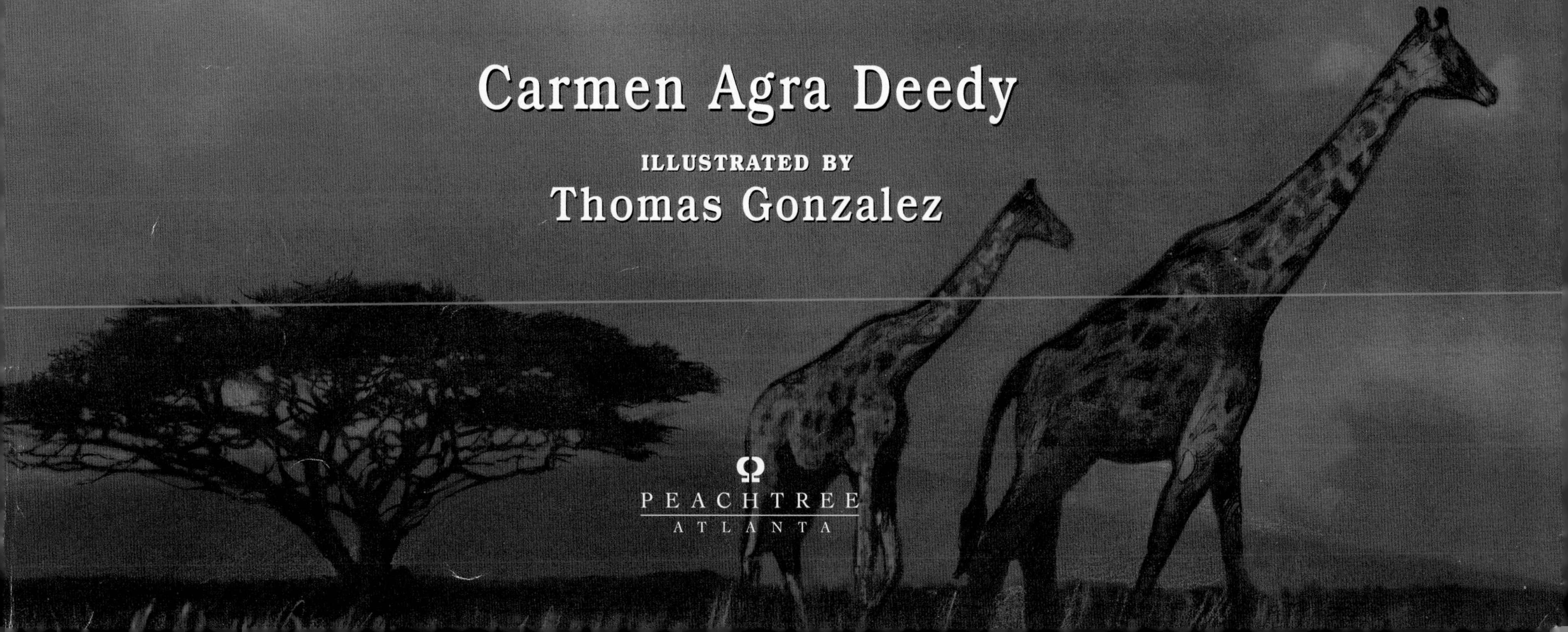

PEACHTREE

ATLANTA

The remote village waits for a story to be told.
News travels slowly to this corner of Kenya.

As Kimeli nears his village,
he watches a herd of bull giraffes
cross the open grassland. He smiles.

He has been away a long time.

A girl sitting under a guava tree sees him first
and cries out to the others. The children run to him
with the speed and grace of cheetahs.
He greets them with a gentle touch on the head,
a warrior's blessing.

The rest of the tribe soon surrounds Kimeli.

These are his people.

These are the Maasai.

Once they were feared warriors.
Now they live peaceably as nomadic cattle herders.
They treat their cows as kindly as they do their children.

They sing to them.
They give them names.
They shelter the young ones in their homes.
Without the herd, the tribe might starve.

To the Maasai, the cow is life.

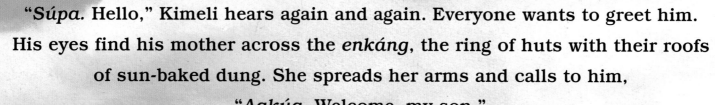

"*Súpa.* Hello," Kimeli hears again and again. Everyone wants to greet him.
His eyes find his mother across the *enkáng*, the ring of huts with their roofs
of sun-baked dung. She spreads her arms and calls to him,
"*Aakúa.* Welcome, my son."

Kimeli sighs.
He is home.

This is sweeter and sadder because
he cannot stay. He must return to the faraway
country where he is learning to be a doctor.

He thinks of New York then.
He remembers September.

A child asks if he has brought any stories.
Kimeli nods.

He has brought with him one story.
It has burned a hole in his heart.

But first he must speak with the elders.

Later, in a tradition as old as the Maasai, the rest of the tribe
gathers under an acacia tree to hear the story.

There is a terrible stillness in the air as the tale unfolds.
With growing disbelief, men, women, and children listen.

Buildings so tall they can touch the sky?
Fires so hot they can melt iron?
Smoke and dust so thick they can block out the sun?

The story ends.
More than three thousand souls are lost.
A great silence falls over the Maasai.

Kimeli waits.
He knows his people.

They are fierce when provoked,
but easily moved to kindness
when they hear of suffering
or injustice.

At last, an elder speaks.
He is shaken, but above all, he is sad.
"What can we do for these poor people?"

Nearby, a cow lows.
Heads turn toward the herd.

"To the Maasai," Kimeli says softly,
"the cow is life."

Turning to the elders,
Kimeli offers his only cow, Enkarûs.
He asks for their blessing.
They give it gladly.
But they want to offer something more.

The tribe sends word to the United States Embassy in Nairobi.
In response, the embassy sends a diplomat.

His jeep jounces along the dusty, rugged roads.
He is hot and tired. He thinks he is going to meet
with Maasai elders. He cannot be more wrong.

As the jeep nears the edge of the village the man sits up.
Clearly, this is no ordinary diplomatic visit.

This is...

...a ceremony.

Hundreds of Maasai greet the American
in full tribal splendor. At the sight of
the brilliant blood-red tunics
and spectacular beaded collars,
he can only marvel.

It is a day of sacred ritual.

Young warriors dance,
leaping into the air like fish from a stream.
Women sing mournful songs.
Children fill their bellies with milk.
Speeches are exchanged.

And now it is time.

Kimeli and his people gather on a sacred knoll, far from the village.
The only sound is the gentle chiming of cowbells.

The elders chant a blessing in Maa
as the Maasai people of Kenya present...

...fourteen cows for America.

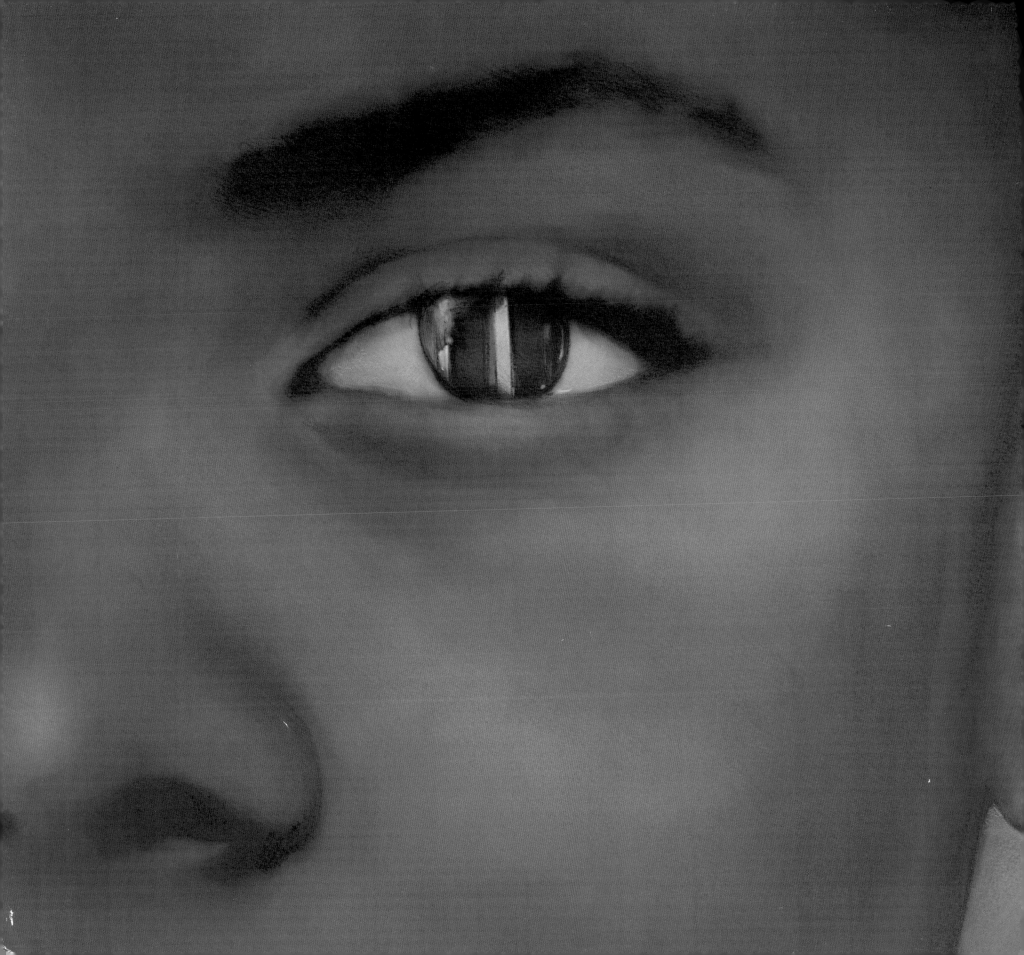

Because there is no nation so powerful it cannot be wounded,

nor a people so small they cannot offer mighty comfort.

A Note from Kimeli Naiyomah

Kimeli (center) with Maasai elders.
Senior chief Ole-Ng'ong'ote (right)
and elder in charge of the warrior camps
Ole-Meleji (left).

JOSH HANER

I am the Kimeli in this story. I grew up in a small village in Kenya.

When I was a little boy my mama said I was too gentle to be a fierce Maasai warrior. I fed little nestlings in the bush and rescued drowning ants from water puddles.

I loved taking care of the cows that belonged to the elders. I felt a close bond with them. A Maasai boy is like one of the calves in the herd. He drinks milk from the cows and feels protected by the bull. My mama was too poor to own a cow. I dreamt of having one someday for my mama and me. It was my biggest dream.

As a young boy, I spent much of my time with the grandpas and grandmas of my tribe. It was through them that I learned my tender warrior heart was not a bad thing. They taught me that the Maasai valued more than strength and boldness. Our ancestors also valued compassion and kindness toward anyone in need: the orphan, the widow, the stranger. To heal the pain in someone's heart, they told me, you give them something that is close to your own heart.

When I was older, I won a scholarship to study in the United States. Many American moms and dads welcomed me to their homes as they would their own child. Like the Maasai elders in my village, these people showed me kindness by taking me in and helping me get an education. America became my second home.

I was in New York City on September 11, 2001. What happened that day was devastating. Many people were left without their mothers and fathers, brothers and sisters. Like countless others, I watched brave firefighters and police officers risk their own lives to save people. My warrior heart could not sit still in me. I wanted to do something to help.

My childhood heart told me what to do: Offer a sacrifice in the way of my people. *To heal a sorrowing heart, give something that is dear to your own.* I had saved enough to fulfill my dream and buy a cow. I decided that the cow, a symbol of life to our people, would be my offering to the grieving Americans. But some pains are too big for one chest to carry. I would ask the elders in my village to bless the cow, to make it special so the gift might take away some of the sadness from American hearts.

I returned to Kenya the following spring and told the story of that tragic day in New York City. Hearing my story, seeing my tears, the ancient spirit of my people was stirred up. When I presented my gift for blessing, others offered up their own precious cows. Fourteen cows were blessed that day. It was a great moment in my village. We were helping to heal a people far away.

When the American ambassador and his wife came to our village to accept the cows, "The Star-Spangled Banner" played over a loudspeaker during the ceremony. Although my people did not understand the song, they stood along with the Americans and placed their hands across their chests. Seeing hundreds of Maasai standing with him in respectful silence made the American diplomat cry. His tears caught the Maasai by surprise, and we were all swept up in the deep emotion of the moment. A connection between the two cultures had been made. We felt we had taken some of America's pain into our Maasai hearts.

These sacred, healing cows can never be slaughtered. They remain in our care in Kenya under the guidance of the revered elder Mzee Ole-Yiampoi. The original fourteen have calved and the herd now numbers over thirty-five. They continue to be a symbol of hope from the Maasai to their brothers and sisters in America. The Maasai wish is that every time Americans hear this simple story of fourteen cows, they will find a measure of comfort and peace.

Wilson Kimeli Ole-Naiyomah

This painting of a special flag commemorating the gift of Maasai cows is on display at the National September 11 Memorial & Museum at the World Trade Center in New York City.

For more details about the story of the 14 cows, please visit *www.14cowsforamerica.com.*

To my children Katie and William,
Erin, and Lauren.
And to my beloved husband, John.
—C. A. D

To my wife Noni and
my daughter Nina.
I am so fortunate to have
both of you in my life.
—T. G.

To all the little children who read
this book. You are the peace
the world has been waiting for.
May you grow to be
compassionate diplomats.
—W. K. N.

Ω

PEACHTREE PUBLISHERS
1700 Chattahoochee Avenue
Atlanta, Georgia 30318-2112
www.peachtree-online.com

Text © 2009 by Carmen Agra Deedy
Illustrations © 2009 by Thomas Gonzalez
Afterword © 2009 by Wilson Kimeli Naiyomah

First trade paperback edition pubished in 2016

Also available in a Spanish-language edition.
14 vacas para América
ISBN 978-1-56145-550-8 (hardcover)
ISBN 978-1-56145-555-3 (trade paperback)

Kimeli Naiyomah, the publisher, and the illustrator wish to thank Josh Haner
for the generous use of his photographs in the development of the illustrations
for this book. The photographs provided invaluable guidance and inspiration for
the accurate depiction of the events described here.

Illustrations created in pastel, colored pencil, and airbrush on 100% rag
archival watercolor paper; text typeset in ITC's Bookman Medium; title
typeset in Linotype's Optima ExtraBlack.

Printed in March 2017 in China by Imago
20 19 18 17 (hardcover)
10 9 8 7 6 5 4 3 2 (trade paperback)

Library of Congress Cataloging-in-Publication Data

Deedy, Carmen Agra.
  14 cows for America / written by Carmen Agra Deedy ; in collaboration
with Wilson Kimeli Naiyomah ;
illustrated by Thomas Gonzalez. — 1st ed.
    p. cm.
  ISBN 978-1-56145-490-7 (hardcover) / 978-1-56145-961-2 (trade paperback)
  1. Kenya—Relations—United States—Juvenile literature. 2. United States—
Relations—Kenya—Juvenile literature. 3. September 11 Terrorist Attacks,
2001—Juvenile literature. 4. Naiyomah, Wilson Kimeli—Juvenile literature. 5.
Masai (African people)—Biography—Juvenile literature. 6. Cows—Kenya—
Juvenile literature. 7. Gifts—Kenya—Juvenile literature. I. Naiyomah, Wilson
Kimeli. II. Gonzalez, Thomas, ill. III. Title.
  E183.8.K4D44 2009

327.676073—dc22

2008055968